EXPORT to EXPLODE
Cash Flow and Profits

*Creating New Streams of Business in
Asia, Africa, and the Americas
with Little Investment*

Lauri E. Elliott

a Leverage Point Strategy™ book
Published by Conceptualee, Inc.

Published by Conceptualee, Inc.:

2015 Ayrsley Town Blvd, Suite 202
Charlotte, North Carolina 28273
United States

ISBN-13 9781453653166

Cover design by Vin Furlong
Copy editing by Iva Cheung

Business & Economics / International / General

"Lauri's book is an authoritative pathfinder, a valuable companion to both the experienced and the new exporter desiring to make the most of opportunities around the globe. It's impressively loaded with facts, tips, and tools. Leverage this book as much as the author wants you to leverage the attractive emerging and frontier markets."

— C. PASCHAL EZE, *Iowa-based author of 11 books, including* Don't Africa Me, For Blacks (and others) Who Really Care, *and* Rebranding Race

"Unlike most writers who limit their topics to the managerial, technical, and logistical aspects of exporting or importing goods and services across international borders, Ms. Elliott also delves into the mindset, strategies, and best practices that should be considered and leveraged to successfully engage in the diverse political, cultural, economic, and social of environments of the various global markets."

— SHELVIN D. LONGMIRE, *Chair, Center for Global Entrepreneurship & Enterprise and EDAC Board of Advisors, Earl G. Graves School of Business & Management, Morgan State University*

There never was a great soul
that did not have some
divine inspiration.

Cicero, 106 BC to 43 BC

*All my work is dedicated to my parents, Elmer
and Alyce, who allowed me to grow and live life
outside of the box.*

Other titles and content on insights and strategy for emerging and global markets can be explored at:

http://www.globalbizconcierge.com

http://www.leveragepointstrategy.com

http://www.globalentrepreneurhandbook.com

http://www.afribiz.info

Table of Contents

Preface

I moved my consulting work from Michigan to Washington, D.C., in the late 1990s in anticipation that the Michigan market was not diversified enough to withstand a major slowdown in the automotive industry. Even today, we can see that the Washington job market is growing while many parts of the U.S. have stagnated.

In 2005 I took a similar step by moving to South Africa, anticipating that emerging markets, particularly Africa, had a lot of untapped potential that would provide many business opportunities in the next ten to 20 years. In 2007 I began to share with colleagues my view that the U.S. was headed for an economic downfall or correction based on what I observed – i.e., extremely over-leveraged consumers as the norm instead of the exception. The global economic crisis came the next year in 2008, and while Western economies contracted, many emerging markets still grew.

Both instances demonstrate what I learned as an entrepreneur – anticipate, proactively respond to, and innovate for emerging business patterns. In many cases, though, I think it is simply logic and common sense. You go where demand is or will be.

What I see now is a new configuration of consumer markets globally and different trade flows, which will require new arrangements of business models even for small to medium-sized enterprises (SMEs) and entrepreneurs. This is really the reason for the current focus of my work and this book. It's not about the technical aspects of exporting. Rather, it's the strategic facets of incorporating exporting into a firm's business model by leveraging available assets to catalyze exporting opportunities and overcome challenges in exporting. The focus is not on large companies or those with a lot of assets but on SMEs. What you will discover are new configurations for doing business successfully to match new market opportunities.

Introduction – Why Export, Why Now?

Exporting, the sale of goods and services to another country, is one of the options for conducting international business. It involves some degree of investment on the part of the exporter to make it work, and it has challenges. However, this book takes the strategic view of exporting as one of many means to expand and sustain business in the long term with short-term and medium-term opportunities and resources available to catalyze a company's export strategy.

The next five years will be a window of opportunity for U.S. exporters to enter emerging markets. So yes, companies should seriously consider exporting, and they should do it now. The question is – why now?

First, the global economic crisis of 2008 and the slow, jobless economic recovery present great challenges for businesses of all sizes. However, in the midst of this period there is another picture of which many U.S. businesses are not aware – emerging markets' growth slowed but continued to grow and rebounded more quickly than developed markets. The imports of developing nations are up 2% above their highs before the economic crisis, while developed nations' import levels are about 19% lower than their highs before the economic crisis, according to the report entitled *A Global Economy with Multiple Growth Poles* by Justin Yiafin Lin. So, while consumer markets in the U.S. and Europe have tightened, they are expanding in developing regions. This is the first reason to consider exporting to emerging markets.

Second, the U.S. became a consumption society instead of an exporting nation. Shifting, or balancing, these two elements is one of many things it will take to get the U.S. economy going. According to the report *Opening Markets, Creating Jobs*, by the U.S. Chamber of Commerce, exporting to countries with which the U.S. has free trade agreements (FTAs) already contributed $1 trillion to the U.S. GDP in 2008. The report also indicates that the FTAs support 17.7 million U.S. jobs and are responsible for 5.4 million U.S. jobs directly.

U.S. firms that export will gain more immediate, direct benefit through the Obama administration's National Export Initiative (NEI), initiated in 2010. The goal of the NEI is to double U.S. exporting within five years with a focus on SMEs, the engine of growth for any economy. There is an increase in resources, support, and momentum in U.S. government organizations, such as EXIM Bank, to assist U.S. firms to export. So, U.S. firms wishing to export can now tap into more support than ever before.

Third, the largest, growing markets for the next 40 years will be those emerging in South America, Africa, and Asia. By starting exports to emerging markets now, U.S. firms will position themselves for long-term growth and sustainability.

So, there is plenty of reason to consider exporting now. However, exporting needs to be incorporated into a company's overall strategy. As you read different parts of this book about leverage points for exporting, consider overall questions for developing an export strategy:

- How does exporting support your overall strategy?
- How can you use an export strategy to expand and sustain your business?

- What local, regional, and global emerging business patterns suggest exporting opportunities for your company in general?
- What markets present the best exporting opportunities?
- What internal capacity and assets can be dedicated to planning and implementing your export strategy?
- What are the short-term and medium-term export opportunities that will catalyze or develop your long-term export strategy?
- What can you use to overcome or minimize challenges in exporting?

Characteristics and Challenges of Exporting

This book is about leveraging to overcome weaknesses, challenges, and obstacles in exporting. However, to properly do so, a business needs to understand the elements involved in exporting. Exporting is one dimension of international business. International business is simply when individuals or firms conduct a business transaction between different countries. International business is divided into three main areas – income, investment, and trade – according to the International Monetary Fund (IMF), which tracks trade across countries.

Income involves return on investment and earnings for creditors, shareholders, and employees. For example, interest payments on debts spanning different countries are income.

Investment involves either direct or portfolio investments. A direct investment is when an investor sets up or acquires, in part or in full, a business in another country. A portfolio investment is investing in financial instruments, either equity or debt.

Trade is when international transactions involve goods or services. Exporting falls within this category. The trading process generally involves three steps: (1) buyer and seller interact before contract, (2) buyer and seller negotiate and sign contract, and (3) the contract is completed and enforced.

Buyer and seller interaction starts with both each searching for the other. The buyer will search channels, including business networks, the Internet, etc., to find a seller for the product or service he or she desires, whereas the seller will make sure that he or she can be found by potential buyers. In the process, both the buyer and seller may learn more about trading between countries.

As the buyer and seller seriously consider completing a contract, there may be samples provided and references requested on both sides. In larger or long-term transactions, buyers and sellers may meet face to face – the buyer may visit the seller's facilities, for example.

Contract negotiations involve providing details on product or service specifications, price, and quality. Also, time and place for delivery and form and time of payment are agreed upon.

When the contract is ready to be signed, both buyer and seller should institute precautions like having payment intermediaries – e.g., an escrow account, a letter of credit, or even PayPal. They should also consider insurance against non-payment or non-performance, if available.

And finally, if the contract is signed and completed but something doesn't work out, buyers and sellers have to consider how to collect on and/or remedy the contract. This may lead to mediation, litigation, or insurance claims.

These international trade transactions can be harder and riskier. You will want to prevent discovering problems after the contract is signed. There are several factors at work in international trade, which make it more complex, so consider the following questions as you work through an export opportunity:

- How does the physical distance, as well as the environmental differences – e.g., cold versus tropical, mountainous versus flat – between countries impact this export opportunity?

- How do the differing political systems between countries impact this export opportunity?

- How do various social and business networks, as well as cultural differences, impact this export opportunity?

- How do the differences in national development, or economic development, between countries impact this export opportunity?

The International Chamber of Commerce (ICC) developed a set of international commercial, or sales, terms. Exporters should manage risk by not agreeing to terms that would hold them responsible for import clearance, including payments, or any other costs or risks at the buyer's end. For example, Delivered Duty Paid (DDP) means you would supply goods or services to a designated place in the country of importation at your own risk and expense. DDP is something you likely want to avoid.

And finally, higher costs are also a consideration for international trade and exporting. Spulber (2007) laid out four types, or "Ts," of costs. The first is tariff and non-tariff costs like regulations that restrict trade and investment, duties on imports, and anti-pollution standards. Second, there is the transaction cost of doing business at a distance, which results from differences in business practices, as well as political, social, and legal climates. Third is the transport cost of getting goods and services to market. And fourth is the time cost, meaning the time that it takes to get a product to market, as well as the lag in communication between agents in the value chain.

Spulber noted that trade and marketing costs can account for the majority of the expense of providing products and services overseas. In the case of manufactured goods, Anderson and van Wincoop (2004) found that trade costs are 170% above the manufacturing cost of a product on average. The trade costs can be broken down as internal costs of trading (55%); cost of crossing borders, including tariffs (44%); transport cost (21%); currency differences (14%); language differences (7%); and other costs like information (9%).

In summary, understanding these challenges and costs of exporting will help you formulate a better export strategy, using leverage points. As you look over the challenges and obstacles faced in exporting, consider the following questions:

- What leverage points can be used to overcome or minimize challenges and obstacles?

- What challenges and obstacles most affect your "go" or "no-go" decision to take an export opportunity?

- Will the "show-stopping" challenges and obstacles change for the better within a year or two during which time you could prepare to export?

- Is the potential reward in exporting significantly larger than the risk?

- Can you limit your risk by scaling back on the initial export strategy and using the first rollout as a staging platform to expand?

Leverage Point 1:
Leverage Point Strategy™

Using the Leverage Point Strategy™ is a leverage point itself. The Leverage Point Strategy™ is a specific methodology, which I developed, based on the concept of leverage. Leverage is the ratio of change in input to the change in output. Greater leverage is gained when a small force multiplies output. The goal is to see a small force produce as much change in output as possible.

Leverage points are those forces, or points, that create the rate of change in output. The power of leverage points is on a continuum from low to high. The best scenario is to locate high leverage points, because, in these cases, the smallest amounts of force effect the greatest change or results.

A very clear picture of a leverage point is the rudder of a ship. It is a small part of the ship in comparison with the size of the ship, but it creates a small force that is able to turn the ship in a new direction. In practical terms, maximizing leverage points makes use of small, but significant, forces.

Leverage points are related to tipping points. A tipping point is a point at which an object is displaced from one place to a new and different state. Leverage points are used to create the tipping point.

Malcolm Gladwell wrote the book *The Tipping Point: How Little Things Make a Big Difference.* He identified three key factors, or types of leverage points, for creating tipping points: the Law of the Few, the Stickiness Factor, and the Power of Context.

The Law of the Few is when a few key types of people champion and catalyze an idea or concept to critical mass. The types of people are Connectors, Mavens, and Salesmen. When all three types of actors advocate an idea, the concept is more likely to reach a tipping point. Connectors, Mavens, and Salesmen are examples of leverage points. Each is a small force that can wield significant results.

The Stickiness Factor is something that sticks in the minds of individuals and influences their behavior in the future. And the Power of Context is when the right environment, or time, aligns with your business opportunity to create momentum.

Each of the leverage points highlighted by Gladwell can induce a tipping point, but it is more likely that the combination of these leverage points will actually force a tipping point.

Another category of leverage points is the types of capital. In essence, these are the strengths you bring to the business opportunity overall. According to Dr. Bruce Cook of Kingdom Venture Capital, there are 13 types of capital:

- **Economic** includes currency, liquid assets, and finance.

- **Social** includes community-focused or social good activities, such as relief work, charity, and scientific research.

- **Spiritual** refers to strength drawn from faith.

- **Knowledge** is what you and your team know, both the intellectual and mental processes.

- **Political** refers to formal political affiliations and influence.

- **Environmental** refers to assets in the global "green" movement, like carbon credits.

- **Creative** includes your creativity, artistic expression, and intellectual property.
- **Positional** refers to the roles, titles, and authority you hold both formally and informally.
- **Institutional** includes formal reputation, influence, status, alliances, and partners.
- **Physical** refers to your body's capacity, including energy and fitness.
- **Generational** refers to legacy, heritage, family lineage, and wealth that are passed down in families.
- **Closeness** refers to the ability to draw close and also to be vulnerable, or open, in relationships.
- **Relational** refers to the span and depth of your relationships both vertically and horizontally.

You may wonder how some types of capital (e.g., social) can serve as leverage points for business, but any form of capital can exert influence over business opportunities. For example, a young African-American attorney, Carlton Owens, moved to Ghana and established a gold mine. His gold mine sits on land on which a local indigenous tribe lives. In addition to getting a mining concession from the government, he had to form an agreement with the local chief on how the operation would benefit the community beyond jobs. Carlton agreed to build a school, among other things. In emerging markets business is not separated from the complex system of society.

In actuality many things are leverage points, including situations and circumstances. However, the leverage point might be in your favor or in someone else's, and the leverage point may have low or high impact. Your goal is to find a series of leverage points in your favor with high-impact potential.

The process of applying the Leverage Point Strategy™ works in conjunction with completing an environmental analysis, as well as a SWOT analysis, of your export opportunity. Following these analyses, apply the Leverage Point Strategy™ by asking yourself the following questions:

- What are the key leverage points that will make this export opportunity work?

- Which of the key leverage points have high, medium, or low impact?

- Which combinations of key leverage points will have the most impact?

- How will the key leverage points help to override the weaknesses and threats in the export opportunity?

- In general, how will I incorporate the high-leverage points and high-leverage-point combinations into the business model?

- How will I know if the leverage points are working?

Once you have applied the Leverage Point Strategy™ to your analysis of the export opportunity, incorporate the leverage points into your business model appropriately. The business model gives a complete picture of how to implement the business, or export, opportunity successfully. It answers the question, "How do you logically create value?" Johann Wallin, in the book *Business Orchestration: Strategic Leadership in the Era of Digital Convergence*, says a business model "defines the value-creation priorities of an actor (business) in respect to the utilization of both internal and external resources. It defines how the actor (business) relates with stakeholders, such as actual and potential customers, employees, unions, suppliers, competitors and other internal groups. It takes account of situations where the actor's (business') activities may (a) affect the business environment and its own business in ways that create conflicting interests, or impose risks on the actor (business) or (b) develop new, previously unpredicted ways of creating value."

In the book *Business Model Generation: A Handbook for Visionaries, Game Changers, and Challengers,* Alexander Osterwalder and Yves Pigneur pose key questions to consider when developing a solid business model. The following is an adaptation focused on leverage points: "What key leverage points will you use to…"

* Activate your customer segments?

* Maximize your revenue streams?

* Improve offerings for your customer segments?

* Better relate to your customers over time?

* Maximize resource allocation to run the business?

* Improve efficiency and effectiveness of key activities in running the business?

* Better utilize and leverage the "people" assets used to run the business?

* Increase and improve outputs of key activities?

* Maximize partnerships, alliances, and collaboration?

* Maximize network and distribution channels to reach customers?

* Manage and reduce costs of running the business?

In summary, leverage points are simply tangible and intangible assets, resources, situations, etc. that can be used to gain and sustain momentum in the business environment. As you analyze a business opportunity or problem, identify leverage points. And use leverage points to help you assess opportunities, as well as incorporate the best leverage points and combinations into the business model and operations.

Leverage Point 2:
Demand-Driven Exporting

According to Lemak and Arunthanes (1997), there are four types of international sales strategies: Domestic-Based Export Strategy, Domestic-Based Value-Added Strategy, Worldwide Value-Added Strategy, and Worldwide Volume Maximization Strategy. In the first two strategies, a firm's focus is on selling to the home market. International sales take only a small portion of a firm's total production, and the firm is therefore not dependent on international sales for sustainability. The difference between the first two strategies is that in the Domestic-Based Value-Added Strategy, more than 10% of a firm's production will occur outside the home country. In the last two international sales strategies, international sales account for more than 30% of a firm's success.

For small businesses and entrepreneurs, the first international sales strategy – Domestic Export-Based Strategy – is typically considered. Lemak and Arunthanes describe this strategy as one in which firms "manufacture or assemble products in the home country to sell in the domestic market...(And) export a small portion of total production to foreign users with little or no modifications via distributors, agents, and/or their own sales subsidiaries." If a firm can find an international market with demand that allows it to sell its products with little or no modification, I would call this a leverage point with potentially high impact. This situation reduces the upfront cost to enter a new market by not having to adapt the product significantly. Another important aspect to exporting is to quickly operate in the black, say within six to 18 months. Small firms typically cannot absorb losses for any great length of time. So, it's also important to find means to generate sales and cash more quickly. Finding markets with high demand and with limited supply is one way to accelerate operating in the black, particularly in emerging markets. *The Financial Times Lexicon* defines *demand* as "the amount of a particular economic good or service that a consumer or group of consumers will want to purchase at a given price."

In emerging markets there is demand for many different things as consumers move up the socioeconomic scale. Even basic services like housing, water access and sanitation, and transport are lucrative markets. For example, housing markets in many African markets like Nigeria, Ghana, and Angola remained strong during the economic crisis. As a whole, construction grew over 12% in Nigeria for each of the last five years, including 2008 and 2009, when the economic crisis hit, according to the *African Statistical Yearbook 2010* by the African Development Bank (ADB).

There are also short-term demand opportunities, which exporters can use to catalyze a long-term strategy. Some businesses saw a golden opportunity to enter the South African market with the 2010 FIFA World Cup. The largest suppliers of the "vuvuzela" horn happened to be Chinese manufacturers like Ninghai Jiying Plastics Manufacturing Company, which exported the vuvuzelas to South Africa. While they barely generated a profit on the vuvuzelas, the Chinese companies can now grow *into* the South African market with other products that have longer-term demand.

In demand-driven exporting, your product or service should readily resonate with your market. If you have a product that is hard to sell, it will take longer to educate the market, reducing or eliminating the advantage you have with the demand-driven opportunity to accelerate sales and cash. Other considerations include how large the demand is and how long it will last. And finally, you also need to remember the "price" aspect of the demand equation. Demand implies that there is a particular price at which high demand is driven. If your price is too high, you reduce the size of your market. And, if the price of the demand is too low for you to make a profit, it may not be the opportunity for you.

In summary, demand-driven exporting is a significant leverage point, which could shape export strategy decisions. Anticipating growing demand in new markets and acting upon this at the right time can strengthen a company's market entry. To flesh out your approach, consider the following questions:

- Where are imports rising by region, country, and/or industry on the whole?

- Where is your sector growing?

- What trends globally, or regionally, suggest that demand for your products or services will grow elsewhere? Where will the demand grow precisely?

- Where is there obvious demand for your product or service?

- Which demand-driven opportunities for exporting will allow you to make little or no modification to your product or service?

- Is the demand-driven opportunity short-, medium-, or long-term?

- Are there any case studies, or examples, of firms in your sector or country that have successfully entered the demand-driven market? What can you learn from these case studies?

- What key challenges do the demand-driven opportunities present?

- What strengths can you leverage to take advantage of the demand-driven opportunities?

- What are the top three demand-driven opportunities, and why did you choose them?

Leverage Point 3:
Consumer Demographics

As with any market opportunity, you need to understand your consumers. There are five cursory demographics with which to explore your export strategy: population, urbanization, gender, age, and socioeconomic status.

The first demographic is the population of a particular country. The idea is to identify volume markets, or markets in which you will likely be able to make a profit or get a return on investment. Volume market considerations may depend on your type of business or sector. For example, a volume market for the Information and Communication Technologies (ICT) sector in Africa is a population greater than 10 million. According to the *World Factbook*, the following is a list of the top fifteen emerging and frontier markets by population in 2010:

1. China (1,330,141,295)

2. India (1,173,108,018)

3. Indonesia (242,968,342)

4. Brazil (201,103,330)

5. Pakistan (177,276,594)

6. Bangladesh (158,065,841)

7. Nigeria (152,217,341)

8. Russia (139,390,205)
9. Mexico (112, 468, 855)
10. Philippines (99,900,177)
11. Vietnam (89,571,130)
12. Ethiopia (88,013,491)
13. Egypt (80,471,869)
14. Turkey (77,804,122)
15. Democratic Republic of Congo (70,916,439)

Urbanization is another demographic consideration. It simply means the percentage of the population that lives in urban areas. For example, 77% of Mexico's people live in urban centers. Since that country has a population of over 100 million, that figure means that over 77 million people are in the urban markets of Mexico.

Urban areas are more concentrated and tend to have better transportation systems than rural areas in emerging markets. These factors can be critical for distributing to and reaching your market. The cost of exporting could be greatly reduced if there are few requirements for in-country transportation beyond the key entry point.

You may also want to consider the rate at which people are moving to urban centers in a country. In a country like Vietnam, with only 28% of its population of 89 million living in urban centers but an approximate 3% rate of urbanization per year, there will be more than 2.6 million new people living in urban centers each year.

Gender is another demographic consideration for your market. Men and women tend to have different spending and shopping patterns. Culture can also impact consumer patterns between men and women. For example, in some Muslim communities women and men are not allowed to mingle openly, so shops adjust for their customers and the culture. Perhaps more significant than gender is age. In many emerging markets, the number of people being born and the number of young people under 40 are greater than in Western markets like the U.S. or Germany. For example, more than 70% of Africa's population is currently 40 or under. Also, regions like Africa will continue to have high growth rates over the next generation. Africa's population is expected to reach over 2 billion in 2050, according to the United Nations Population Division. This will exceed the population of countries like China and India.

Finally, you need to consider what the socioeconomic status of your market is. While there is a large, growing middle class in emerging markets, consumers there do not have the purchasing power of consumers in Western markets, which generally exceeds $30,000 per year per consumer. The annual purchasing power of a Chinese consumer was $6,600 (and $3,100 for an Indian consumer) in 2010, according to the *World Factbook*.

Another socioeconomic indicator, which can be used to look at consumers in emerging markets, is the rate at which they are moving up the socioeconomic scale. If you have 10% of a population of 20 million moving up the socioeconomic scale to the next level in five years, this means 2 million will have more money to spend in the medium-term.

This indicator is also important because it is known that people's spending patterns change as they move up the socioeconomic scale. For example, people change their food consumption patterns to include more meat and dairy as they move up.

In summary, demographics you can use to spot initial strengths and possible sustainability of opportunities include population, urbanization, gender, age, and socioeconomic indicators. To flesh out your understanding of demographics as a leverage point, consider the following questions:

- How large is the population in the emerging market?
- Is the market large enough to support your sales and return-on-investment goals?
- What percentage of the population lives in urban centers?
- What are the differences between men and women in the market, and how might they impact sales?
- What is the buying power of the consumer market?
- What are the consumption patterns of the market?
- What is the age distribution of the market?
- What basic needs or services are not being met adequately for the consumers?
- What are the consumer markets like in surrounding countries?
- What consumption patterns can be anticipated in the medium-term or long-term as the population increases in buying power?

Leverage Point 4:
Language and Culture

Language is a critical consideration when looking where to export. Imagine trying to get simple directions from someone who doesn't speak your language. Now apply that to doing business in a foreign country in another language. While the task is not impossible, you put yourself at a distinct disadvantage. Entering markets that speak the same language as you do is a leverage point in your favor.

The top five most spoken languages in the world are Chinese, Spanish, English, Arabic, and Hindi, according to *Ethnologue.com*. For business communication, English and French are quite universal.

In emerging markets some of the countries in which English is an official language include Hong Kong, Singapore, India, Philippines, Pakistan, and Sri Lanka, according to the *World Factbook*. In Africa over 20 countries, including Nigeria, Kenya, South Africa, Botswana, Tanzania, and Ghana, have English as an official language. In North America many Caribbean states/territories like Puerto Rico, U.S. Virgin Islands, Jamaica, and the Bahamas also have English as an official language.

You can also look at countries with multiple official languages; these may serve as a springboard into surrounding, non-English-speaking countries. How? In territories like Hong

Kong, which is a part of China, people often speak multiple languages. If the people with whom you work in Hong Kong both speak Chinese and understand the culture of mainland China, they can possibly serve as intermediaries for you to access the large market on mainland China.

In Egypt, English is not official, but it is widely understood, and Arabic is an official language. Because of this, Egypt could be a springboard into the markets of the Middle East and North Africa (MENA), which have Arabic, but not English, as an official language. And Rwanda, located in East/Central Africa and in which both French and English are official languages, may provide linkages between French-speaking and English-speaking African nations.

For small enterprises entering non-English-speaking markets, the key criterion is to have competent and trustworthy people representing you and looking out for your interests. Typically, you will only be able to assess the quality of your associates as you work with them and develop the relationships. Another approach is to have a high-trust relationship with an English-speaking individual, or organization, who has strong, trusted partners that can be held accountable in the market of interest.

As you expand your interest in exporting, you may consider language and culture immersion for key people in your organization over which you have more influence and who have your company's interest, as well as their own, at heart. For China, one resource to learn about its culture, arts, and language is the Confucius Institute, which has branches all over the world.

As mentioned before, determining whether you have trustworthy and competent associates is worth the effort to confirm because of the potential risk associated with not getting it right. In fact, this aspect is important to consider whether the export market is English- or non-English-speaking.

However, the issue with trust may be not only whether a person is trustworthy but also whether *you* have the ability to trust that person. Both aspects are important for building relationships necessary for exporting. Culture can be a significant factor in developing trust relationships with competent associates. Humans tend to trust people that are similar to themselves – those who have similar backgrounds, have similar socioeconomic status, or come from the same in-group. Professor Geert Hofstede said that "culture is more often a source of conflict than synergy." A nation's culture can broadly be understood along five cultural dimensions, which according to Hofstede are:

- **Power distance** – the degree to which less powerful members of society find it acceptable or expect power to be unequal.

- **Individualism** – the degree to which a society is individualistic versus collectivistic.

- **Masculinity** – how roles are distributed between men and women in the society.

- **Uncertainty and avoidance** – the degree to which a society can deal with uncertainty and ambiguity.

- **Long-term orientation** – the degree to which a society has a long-term or short-term outlook.

While differences in culture tend to promote conflict rather than synergy, a savvy exporter will come to learn the differences and adapt to them to maximize opportunities. In fact, those differences may prove highly useful to you. For example, in Brazil the business culture embraces collaboration, an important facet of teamwork and building strong ecosystems. This is an asset you can use if you have Brazilian partners to strengthen your international business ecosystem.

Finally, while it might be more costly or risky to export to countries with language and cultural differences from your own, you may find that the opportunity is worth the risk. As you are exploring an exporting opportunity, doing a risk–reward analysis

is called for. The following questions will help you work through
the issue, or leverage point, of language and culture, which will
contribute to your understanding of the risks and rewards:

- Which emerging countries speak the native tongue of
  your business?

- Are there certain countries, in which multiple languages
  are spoken, that you could use as a springboard into
  other countries and surrounding region?

- What businesspeople do you know who fluently speak the
  language of the market you want to enter?

- Will differences in language and culture mean
  modifications, small or large, to your product, such as
  different labeling and instructions?

- What are the additional costs and risks associated with
  entering a market using a different language?

- Is the opportunity in the market with a different language
  significantly more than those in English-speaking
  emerging markets?

- How can you use other leverage points or strengths to
  compensate for the difference in language?

- Do you have a competent and trustworthy organization,
  or person, that can bridge the language and culture
  difference?

- If you are still hedging on the risk of the non-English-
  speaking market, are there several English-speaking
  countries you could enter simultaneously to match the
  opportunity in the non-English-speaking market?

- Can you stage your export strategy to English-speaking
  countries first, then expand to non-English-speaking
  countries?

- How is the host country's culture similar to and different
  from American culture?

- How can you work around the cultural differences in the host country?
- How can you build on the cultural similarities in the host country?
- Who can help you navigate the culture in the host country?

Leverage Point 5:
Cities and Economic Hubs

In the early 1800s only 7% of the world's population lived in urban centers. Today over half of the world's population lives in urban centers. In 2050 about 70% of the world's population is expected to live in urban centers, according to the United Nations. The concentration of population into smaller areas offers entrepreneurs access to a larger market in a smaller geographic space.

Megacities are those with populations of more than 10 million. According to the *Principal Agglomerations of the World* by Thomas Brinkhoff, the top megacities in 2010 (and their populations) in emerging markets are:

1. Canton, China (24,200,000)

2. Mexico City, Mexico (24,200,000)

3. Delhi, India (23,400,000)

4. Mumbai, India (22,800,000)

5. Sao Paolo, Brazil (20,900,000)

6. Manila, Philippines (19,600,000)

7. Shanghai, China (18,400,000)

8. Calcutta, India (16,300,000)

9. Karachi, Pakistan (16,200,000)

10. Jakarta, Indonesia (15,400,000)
11. Cairo, Egypt (15,200,000)
12. Beijing, China (13,600,000)
13. Dhaka, Bangladesh (13,600,000)
14. Moscow, Russia (13,600,000)
15. Buenos Aires, Argentina (13,300,000)
16. Istanbul, Turkey (12,800,000)
17. Tehran, Iran (12,800,000)
18. Rio de Janeiro, Brazil (12,600,000)
19. Lagos, Nigeria (11,800,000)

Another variable to consider is the rate of urbanization. If the rate of urbanization is positive, it means the consumer markets will enlarge in cities. For example, Pakistan has a rate of urbanization close to 5%. Karachi, a city with a population over 22 million, will grow by at least one million new people each year.

A challenge for many fast-growing cities is not having sufficient services – transport, housing, water, etc. Throughout history, even in places like New York City, informal settlements arose to take in new city dwellers. With these new settlements comes a strain on existing services, hitting both formal and informal settlements. This can cause problems for businesses that also need services. Power outages caused by overloading is one example.

However, this situation also creates unique opportunities for entrepreneurs who possess alternative means to provide services that the government cannot, such as clean water, energy, housing, and transport.

In addition to cities, economic hubs also offer tremendous opportunities. An economic hub is a concentrated area in and through which economic activity flows. If you identify a good hub, you can create new opportunities that flow to places with which the hub is connected.

In Africa Nigeria serves as the major economic hub for West Africa. Egypt is the key economic hub for North Africa. Kenya serves as the key economic hub for East Africa. And South Africa is the major economic hub for Southern Africa.

South Africa generates about 20% of the economic activity for the entire African continent. Within South Africa the Gauteng Province is the economic hub for the country, with about 30% of economic activity centered there. Gauteng Province serves as a key economic hub not only for South Africa but also for the entire continent. In a recent news article published by the *Times* in South Africa, Mudunwazi Baloyi, General Manager of Investment, Trade and Projects Facilitation of the Gauteng Economic Development Agency (GEDA), said that Gauteng is the fourth-largest economy in Africa, after the countries of South Africa, Egypt, and Nigeria.

Both cities and economic hubs have another distinct advantage: they generally have more and better business services and supporting sectors. I like to call Sandton, a suburb of Johannesburg in Gauteng Province, the "Wall Street" or "Manhattan" of Africa. Inside the few square miles of Sandton's central business district is a great concentration of financial and economic activity, and multinational firms and visitors/representatives from almost every country can be found. Many of the largest and most significant business, political, and social conferences, workshops, and forums for the continent are held in Sandton.

In addition, Pretoria, Gauteng, has a large number of embassies and consulates, representing countries from all over the world. Generally, each country will have representatives that deal with commercial and economic interests housed in the embassy or consulate. So, from one economic hub a large number of regional and global business interests can be accessed.

And finally, as you look at cities and economic hubs, also take note of whether their concentration is growing or dispersing. In other words, are economic activity, workers, and capital increasingly concentrating in the area, or are they declining? This will help you look at the potential of using cities and economic hubs as a leverage point in the medium- to long-term. And to flesh out your understanding of cities and hubs as a leverage point for your exporting opportunity, consider the following questions:

- What are the key cities and economic hubs in the emerging market of interest?

- What key industries and sectors are represented in the city or economic hub?

- Are there basic services that are not being met and that you could provide?

- What multinational firms are present in the city or economic hub?

- How do trade and services flow in and out of the city or economic hub?

- What other markets does the city or economic hub open up to you?

- What are the underserved markets in the city or economic hub?

- Are there sufficient business services and supporting sectors like transport to make it easier to do business when working with a local partner?

- Are there any major constraints for business in the city or economic hub? How do you overcome them?

- What particular aspects of the city or economic hub can be leveraged?

Leverage Point 6:
Economic Zones and Clusters

Economic zones are geographic areas designated to promote trade and economic development within a country. They have more liberalized economic policies than the countries in which they reside, and these policies are highly conducive to both native and foreign business. Typical advantages for businesses and investors include tax incentives, better infrastructure, better institutions, better processes, and freer flow of international trade.

There are different forms of economic zones, from free ports to information-processing zones. Some economic zones around the globe include Hyderabad, New Delhi, and Pune in India; Subic and Bataan in the Philippines; and Dubna and Lipetsk in Russia.

China's growth story is very tied to the introduction of economic zones in the 1980s. For example, the Shenzhen Export Processing Zone was a small village and has now grown to almost the size of a megacity with around 9 million people. Not only are economic zones often better places to conduct business, but they may also offer the chance of a growing market for exporters.

Another model for concentrating and leveraging economic activity is clusters, most notably researched and introduced by Michael Porter. A cluster is a group of enterprises in close geographic proximity that produce similar or related products in a particular field – e.g., nanotechnology, leather, diamonds, etc. In Uganda there are over 20 diverse clusters under development. Globally, nations are seeing clusters as a means to spur economic development. For exporters, they may offer alliances, bringing expertise, value chains, and capacity, in a foreign country.

One of the models for economic clusters is Silicon Valley in San Jose, California. This technology cluster has created an ecosystem that drives technology innovation around the globe. Note that successful clusters also can spur connections with other markets and multinationals, such as the case with the automotive clusters in India. In the Chennai-Hosur-Bangalore region cluster, Toyota, Mitsubishi, Hyundai and Ford are among the multinationals involved.

In essence, economic zones and clusters serve as pathways for exporters to enter new markets through the inherent strengths they bring. An exporter can find expertise and ecosystems to support its singular effort to enter new markets while containing the strain on existing resources.

While country analysis is important for determining an opportunity to export, taking a closer look at the strengths of specific economic zones or clusters within a country may help you discover leverage points in favor of exporting to that country even when the overall country analysis indicates that the business climate there is weak. To flesh out your understanding of using economic zones and clusters as leverage points, consider the following questions:

- What economic clusters or zones exist in the emerging economy of interest?
- Which economic clusters or zones align with your business strategy?

- What is the experience of others in the economic cluster or zone of interest?

- Are there other companies from the U.S. present or involved in the economic cluster or zone?

- What incentives are provided in the economic zone? How does this improve the opportunity for you?

- At what stage of development is the economic cluster or zone? Is its development sufficient to prove useful to you?

- Are there firms within the cluster or zone you could tap as clients?

- What is the rate of increased economic activity and population around the economic zone or cluster? Is this in itself a market to consider?

- Can you offer services or products that are needed by firms in an economic zone or cluster?

- Are there firms with which you can partner or align in the economic zone or cluster?

Leverage Point 7:
Trade and Investment Agreements

A trade agreement is one between two or more parties, possibly covering a wide range of tax, tariff, trade, and investment issues. In bilateral agreements between two countries like Canada and South Africa, there are preferential and protection measures that benefit businesses from both countries. Along with trade agreements, business councils are mandated by governments to represent the private sector. In some sense they are similar to chambers of commerce.

Exporters can incorporate the preferential and protection measures in trade agreements to leverage opportunities in a specific country. Typical concerns of those doing business overseas include the following: How easy is it to remove money from the host country? What protection is there for assets in the host country? These and other issues may be covered by trade or investment agreements.

With exporting, however, an exporter will often place the burden of issues pertaining to the host country on the local partner or distributor as much as possible. For example, instead of stocking inventory in the country under the exporter's ownership, the local partner or distributor is required to purchase the inventory.

Trade agreements also bring opportunities to network, since businesses generally form part of the diplomatic delegations accompanying government officials to discuss trade agreements. For example, President Jacob Zuma of South Africa recently took along over 350 businesspeople on his state visit to China. This offers businesses unique access to people and organizations in the host country.

Also, business councils serve as excellent channels to gain information, contacts, and expertise on operating in a foreign country. In a recent example, I had a person approach me who needed very specific information about getting a product through customs in Algeria. I contacted the U.S.–Algeria Business Council, and they were readily able to identify the organization that could assist. For someone trying to retrieve this information on his or her own, the process could have taken several weeks.

The U.S. has bilateral agreements with emerging economies in the G20 like Argentina, Russia, and Turkey. To learn about U.S. trade agreements, contact the U.S. Commercial Service, which provides a lot of resources and support for exporters. You can also check with the United Nations Conference on Trade and Development (UNCTAD), which keeps a list of bilateral and investment agreements in place for each country.

Trade agreements can serve as key leverage points, owing to the ecosystems developed to support them. However, you will need to explore any trade agreement in sufficient detail so that you understand its benefits, limitations, and implications. While you are exploring trade and investment agreements as leverage points, consider the following questions:

- What trade agreements does the U.S. hold with the emerging economy of interest?

- What aspect of those trade agreements can you leverage for your business?

- What protection does the trade agreement offer?

- Are there any initiatives developed through the trade agreement in which you should be involved?

- Are there business opportunities arising out of initiatives evolving from the trade agreement?

- What business opportunities have been identified for businesses in the U.S. through the trade agreement?

- Who are the key stakeholders of whom you should be aware?

- Which trade agreements tied to the host country will also help your business enter other markets?

- Who can you consult that has intimate knowledge of the trade agreements?

- How will specific trade agreements allow you to leverage other strengths?

Leverage Point 8:
Regional Economic Communities

Like economic hubs, regional economic communities (RECs) can provide a strategic focus for businesses and investors. RECs focus on creating at least a free trade area, customs union, and common market between member countries. While this helps the member countries with cross-border trade and opens markets to the world, it also provides larger and more varied opportunities for businesses and investors.

The European Union (EU) is a prime example. The *World Factbook* says the population of the EU is close to 500 million in 2010, compared with about 85 million in Germany, its most populated member state. The purchasing power of 500 million people is obviously greater than that of 85 million.

The goal of an REC is to make the movement of factors of production, as well as goods and services, between member countries as easy as within the countries. This will guarantee efficient resource use, which is a competitiveness factor that can attract investment and boost economic growth. For exporters and entrepreneurs, it means that a free trade agreement in the REC will allow your products to move from one country to another with few or no tariffs and make it easier for you to reach across borders within the region to expand your market.

As an example, if you planned to concentrate your business and investment ventures in the East Africa economic hub of Kenya, you would greatly benefit from the ICT infrastructure and institutions developed for the East Africa Community (EAC). The EAC consists of Burundi, Kenya, Rwanda, Tanzania, and Uganda. It has a combined population of about 136 million, compared with about 40 million in Kenya alone. For those who do business and invest in consumer markets, the difference in market potential based on size is significant.

RECs can also help business more successfully navigate within many countries simultaneously by harmonizing policies, incentives, etc., between member states. For example, the EAC is working on a regional investment code, which means foreign businesses and investors will have one code to engage with, as opposed to five.

Detractors of the U.S. experience with the North American Free Trade Agreement (NAFTA) have claimed that it has served as a means for jobs to be exported so that companies could pay less for labor. However, services or products that can be reproduced elsewhere by someone else with cheaper labor will not help sustain either your business or the U.S. economy, because these services or products have a high probability of being substituted.

The key for exporters is to develop competitive products and services with a low likelihood of substitution. This can lead to more jobs in your home country and contribute to the nation's bottom line.

Innovation is key to sustainability. If your company is not innovative, exporting will not solve your long-term sustainability issues.

In summary, RECs enlarge market potential for exporters automatically and can make it easier to navigate exporting to several countries simultaneously. However, it is important to identify the specific benefits and limitations of an REC in the case of your exporting opportunity. As you explore RECs as leverage points, consider the following questions:

- In which regional economic communities, or free trade agreements, does the emerging market of interest participate?

- What are the market size and characteristics of the regional economic community for your sector and industry?

- What additional opportunities does the regional economic community bring to you?

- Does the U.S. have direct agreements with the regional economic community?

- What other trade agreements does the regional economic community have with other countries or regions? How can you benefit from those?

- In which country in the regional economic community should you start?

- How can you use regional economic communities to leverage your other strengths?

- Can you consult other firms in the U.S. that are doing a lot of business in the regional economic community?

- What is the economic outlook for the regional economic community in question?

- What factors – e.g., tariffs, border crossing, and transport – within the regional economic community still present challenges for cross-border trade? How can you work around them?

Leverage Point 9:
Diplomatic Missions

The network of diplomatic missions involving the U.S. and the country you would like to enter to do business provides a wealth of on-the-ground, up-to-date information. As an example, the U.S. Commercial Service agency places a specialist in many U.S. embassies abroad. Every few years they produce guides providing information for U.S. businesses on doing business in foreign countries.

Even if information is not posted on the Internet, be assured that U.S. embassies abroad and foreign embassies in the U.S. normally have commercial liaisons specifically dedicated to promoting business. These commercial liaisons can locate information and contacts in the emerging market of interest. A U.S. embassy will often have a list of suggested service organizations for both personal and business concerns. However, they typically provide a disclaimer that they do not endorse anyone on the list, and you are responsible for doing your own due diligence.

Embassies can also help with basic due diligence by certifying that businesses in their home country are legitimately established entities and may provide some indication of standing within the country. However, do not expect them to do a thorough background check. When you are considering large transactions, you need to employ additional due diligence services from accountants, lawyers, etc.

Diplomatic missions are also involved in trade delegations to and from their country. If you are local to any of these establishments, it would be good to check for events at which you can interact with businesspeople from the country of interest.

Diplomatic missions also serve as the voice of their country's government abroad. Foreign embassies are able to provide you with information and access to government departments and officials covering policy and regulations that may impact your export opportunity.

To locate a U.S. embassy and foreign embassies in the U.S., check with the U.S. State Department. There are a few resources online like Embassy World, which list embassies globally, but the information may not be the most up-to-date.

In summary, diplomatic missions should be one of your primary sources for collecting initial information, because the resources are provided free in many instances. Also, diplomatic missions have information that reflects the local atmosphere and context in which to do business. Note that the perspective given from government agencies or diplomatic missions is useful but may not fully reflect the business context. That's why it is important to use several different sources to gain a better picture of the emerging market that you want to enter. As you explore diplomatic missions as leverage points, consider the following questions:

- Who are the commercial attachés at the embassy of the emerging market of interest in the U.S.?

- Does the embassy put out regular communication about the business climate and opportunities?

- Does the embassy maintain a list of recommended business associates related to your interest?

- With what information or contacts can the embassy assist you?

- What are the procedures for the embassy to verify the legitimacy of an enterprise or investment opportunity in its country?

- What major projects and priority sectors in the emerging market can you tap into?

- In what business-related projects and initiatives is the U.S. involved in the emerging economy of interest?

- How can the U.S. diplomatic mission in the emerging economy of interest help you?

- How can you use diplomatic missions to leverage your strengths?

- How do the diplomatic missions interact with business groups like chambers?

Leverage Point 10:
Chambers of Commerce
and Business Councils

Many entrepreneurs are familiar with local chambers of commerce but don't often realize that they exist in almost every country worldwide. A chamber of commerce is simply an association of businesspeople who protect and promote business interests. Chambers create networks of local, regional, national, and international businesspeople that can be tapped into for information, resources, expertise, and even partnership. Chambers also often serve a vital role as the voice of the business community with governments.

As a first step, check with local chambers in your area to identify affiliations they might have with chambers and other organizations in foreign countries. For example, I discovered that my local chamber had strong relationships with organizations in the United Kingdom and Germany. They also make trips abroad to promote business for the city.

If a local chamber has programs and affiliations that seem as though they might be fruitful for you, absorb as much as you can from it. As you collect information, this will help you draw potential pathways to get to your market. Don't forget to use the same approach and check with regional and national chambers that may have a greater variety of initiatives focused on emerging markets and international trade.

Business councils are similar to chambers in that they serve as the voice of the business community. However, they are often formed at the behest of a government trying to make sure they stay connected to key stakeholders. Bilateral or multilateral business councils are a good example. These business councils are formed as a result of bilateral or multilateral trade agreements being reached between nations. They have a unique strength of being directly connected with the business community of the host country. For example, there is the U.S.–Angola Business Council.

The foremost chamber in the world is the International Chamber of Commerce (ICC), which has taken on the role of not only promoting and protecting business interests but also developing practices and standards for international business. ICC also provides model templates for international contracts and agreements and standards in arbitration and dispute resolution.

And finally, you can contact local chambers in the emerging market in which you are interested. This is sometimes more of a challenge because not all of them have listed website or email addresses. I found that the best approach, yielding the fastest results, is to call the chamber by phone. Today, the cost of a call to most countries is quite reasonable. The World Chambers Directory, published by the World Chambers Federation, is a list of many chambers worldwide.

A special note: ICC and the Junior Chamber of Commerce (JCC) have branches in several different countries. There are also regional umbrella chambers for chambers of commerce in a specific region like the Pan-African Chamber of Commerce. And, the U.S. Chamber of Commerce has branches in foreign countries.

In summary, chambers of commerce and business councils are excellent sources of information and connections. To leverage these available assets, consider the following questions:

- What local chambers are involved in emerging market activities?
- To which overseas chambers are local and national chambers connected?
- What are the chambers in the emerging market of interest?
- Are there any chambers or industry associations specifically focused on your industry?
- What preliminary market, industry, or sector information can the chambers in the host country provide?
- Who do the chambers in the host country recommend to assist with exploring the export opportunity and operational requirements?
- How can you use the chambers to connect with key stakeholders and partners, as well as build your ecosystem or value chain?
- How can you use chambers to leverage your other strengths?
- What significant events hosted by the chamber should you attend?
- Are there any initiatives sponsored by the chambers in which you should participate?

Leverage Point 11:
Multinational and
Micro-Multinational Corporations

Multinational corporations (MNCs) are those that do business across borders and/or have operations in different countries. MNCs are typically associated with very large firms like HP, Unilever, Cadbury, and Toyota.

There are three advantages to entrepreneurs in emerging markets with high concentrations of MNCs. First, entrepreneurs can learn of unique cultural and market issues from MNC representatives, particularly those from their own country. Second, if MNCs have a large number of expatriates who work in a country, this creates a market in itself to explore. Third, MNCs can provide strategic complements for your business venture through knowledge spillovers, potential industry or business spinoffs, pools of specialized skilled labor, etc. For example, South Africa has a strong ICT sector with U.S. multinationals like Microsoft, Cisco, Intel, and HP as major stakeholders in the national and regional market.

There are several different sources for identifying MNCs in a particular country. First, check with your country's embassy/consulate in that country. Typically, large MNCs will register their assets with the embassy. Second, the host country's department of trade normally tracks foreign firms. Third, Dun and Bradstreet maintains a list of multinationals and their affiliates in foreign countries in the "Who Owns Whom" database.

Micro-multinational corporations are newer forms of organizations referring to start-ups and SMEs that operate across borders. The age of ICT and mobility has made it possible for these firms to operate cost effectively across borders. Micro-multinationals are prevalent in the ICT sector. When you conduct international business in at least two countries and are a small business, you are a form of micro-multinational corporation.

Micro-multinational is also a name attached to small firms that outsource part of their work overseas, primarily through online freelance and outsourcing platforms like Elance and oDesk. Firms that service micro-multinationals in this way offer a distinctive advantage that entrepreneurs can use to minimize the cost of activities – such as doing their online research, setting up and maintaining their websites, etc. – that are focused on international sales. Entrepreneurs find a competitively priced marketplace for talent. You can also hire the professionals to work on a regular, project-by-project, or ad hoc basis. This is a tool to make your cash go much further.

As with any online or overseas transactions, consider the appropriateness of the task. Sensitive or confidential business information may not be suitable for contracting or outsourcing. Gauge the risk of harm to your firm if the work being outsourced is shared or if confidentiality is breached. If it would cause significant harm, limit the amount of data shared through outsourcing, to make it difficult for anyone to get a clear picture of your business model, intellectual property, or clients. Most offenders want it to be easy.

You can always adapt your criteria for information shared as your trust for individuals increases. However, it's critical to protect your interests sufficiently while maintaining an open atmosphere to do business. An open business environment is excellent, and it is naturally attached to today's business context; however, you still need to protect your firm against external shocks.

In summary, the multinational corporation ecosystem is a good platform to investigate how business is done in another country through the eyes of people who come from the U.S. They have unique experiences with both the U.S. and the host country. Also, organizing your firm as a micro-multinational may bring additional opportunities and capacities while making cost-effective use of current resources. To investigate using multinational corporation ecosystems and micro-multinational organizational forms as leverage points, consider the following questions:

- Is there a good number of multinationals operating in the country of interest?

- What multinationals from the host country operate in the U.S.?

- What multinationals from the U.S. operate in the host country?

- What can you learn from the experience of multinationals involved with the emerging economy of interest?

- What channels and ecosystems offered by the multinational corporations can you tap into?

- Can you target multinationals or their staff as clients?

- How can you use multinationals to leverage your strengths?

- How can you use ICT to build your exporting value chain in the emerging economy?

- How can you use outsourcing services to support your export strategy?

Leverage Point 12:
Export-Focused Organizations

Typically, governments will have divisions focused on exporting issues for business. In the U.S. this function is managed through several different agencies, including EXIM Bank and the U.S. Commercial Service. Governmental bodies provide information, resources, technical assistance, and finance for exporters. Export organizations sponsored by the government will often be found at the state level also.

Export councils also provide export assistance. Export councils often fill the gap between government export assistance and what is needed by exporters, particularly new exporters. You will often find a synergistic relationship between export councils and governments, which is beneficial for exporters.

Export councils are typically industry bodies that help firms in specific industries export their products. For example, in South Africa there is the Automotive Industry Export Council (AIEC), which is a part of the National Association of Automotive Manufacturers of South Africa (NAAMSA). In India an example is the Plastics Export Promotion Council (PLEXCONCIL). In Brazil SOFTEX is the agency that promotes export of Brazilian software technology. And the U.S. has the U.S. Dairy Export Council. Also in the U.S. are general export councils, such as the National District Export Council.

The benefit of working with industry export councils is that they not only focus on exports from your country but also understand the issues specific to your industry as it relates to exporting. In the case of SOFTEX in Brazil, they also represent the interest of the industry abroad by making others more aware of the strengths of the Brazilian software industry. Export councils will provide specific initiatives and programs to support product and service export, as well as provide technical assistance for getting it done.

From the private sector, there are firms that specialize in exporting. First, there are exporters within your country that will take your product on as an offering and market your product abroad through their channels. This is called indirect exporting. The benefit for you is not having to deal with the complexity of an overseas market. The downside is that you do not develop your own capacity or channels for exporting.

If you take command of your own export program, you will likely work with a freight forwarder. While cargo shipping is at the heart of the forwarding industry, many can handle the whole spectrum of logistics, including warehousing. In some cases freight forwarders can even help you locate trade financing. Essentially, they become your export agent.

As a final note, if you are new to exporting, you should begin by learning about the export process. The U.S. Department of Commerce produces *A Basic Guide to Exporting*. The 1998 edition is available online for free. Also, as you explore export-focused organizations as leverage points, consider the following questions:

- What are the local exporting support organizations in the government and private sector?

- Are there exporters in your local area or state from which you can learn?

- What industry-specific exporting organizations exist?

- How can the host country's investment promotion agency assist you?
- What government export programs can you access?
- What additional exporting resources are available to you?
- How can you use export-focused structures to leverage your opportunity in an emerging economy?
- Which export services, consultants, and platforms fit your needs and export strategy?
- What internal capacity do you need to take advantage of the export opportunity?

Conclusion

This book is a guide for SMEs to take advantage of market opportunities by incorporating exporting into their business models and leveraging available assets to ignite expanding opportunities. While exporting comes with a myriad of challenges, the rewards can be well worth the efforts to overcome them.

U.S. businesses have a unique window of opportunity in the next five years to enter emerging markets. There is now, more than ever before, an exciting opportunity to capture the growth markets of countries once considered non-desirable in developing regions.

America's economy is struggling. Exporting is an option to improve the economy and your own business. Research shows that exporting companies typically are more competitive than domestic-only firms, and exporting companies, in spite of popular belief, do create jobs. This is only enhanced by the current National Export Initiative to double U.S. exporting within five years.

By starting exports to emerging markets now, U.S. firms can position themselves for long-term growth and sustainability.

Key Points

To learn how to take advantage of the opportunities and to overcome the challenges, use the following key points to develop a Leverage Point Strategy™:

- Consider your leverage points.
- Weigh the risks and rewards.
- Determine how you can use language as a leverage point in countries where people speak the same language as you.
- Learn how to use cultural similarities and differences as leverage points.
- Study consumer demographics in your targeted emerging countries.
- Look at the concentration of population in areas that offer access to a larger market in a smaller geographic space. Study what's lacking, what businesses and services are available, what you believe are the major constraints and how they can be overcome, and how certain aspects can be leveraged.
- Research economic zones and clusters and the advantages for businesses and investors regarding tax incentives, infrastructure, institutions, processes, and easier flow of international trade.

- Learn how to leverage trade agreements and regional economic communities.

- Use U.S. diplomatic missions and chambers of commerce and those of the country you would like to enter as resources for information.

- Study how you can take advantage of emerging markets with higher concentrations of multinational corporations.

- Use export-focused organizations as a resource.

- Understand the characteristics, elements, and challenges of exporting.

Resources

The following is a list of (mostly free) resources on exporting that you may find useful:

- American Chambers Abroad – http://www.uschamber.com/international/directory/default
- *A Basic Guide to Exporting* 1998 (updated version available for purchase) – http://www.unzco.com/basicguide/
- **Bonus Material for Book** – bookbonus@conceptualee.com
- City Populations – http://www.citypopulation.de
- Embassy World – http://www.embassyworld.com
- Freelance/Outsourcing Platforms – http://www.guru.com; http://www.freelancer.com; http://www.elance.com; http://www.odesk.com
- International Chamber of Commerce (ICC) – http://www.iccwbo.org
- International Monetary Fund (IMF) – http://www.imf.org
- International Trade and Tariff Data – http://www.wto.org/english/res_e/statis_e/statis_e.htm
- National Cultural Orientation Comparisons – http://www.geert-hofstede.com/hofstede_dimensions.php
- National District Export Council U.S. – http://www.districtexportcouncil.com/

- Resources for Doing Business and Investing in Emerging Markets – http://www.afribiz.info; http://www.globalbizconcierge.com

- *Trade Finance Guide: A Quick Reference for U.S. Exporters* – http://trade.gov/media/publications/abstract/trade_finance_guide2008desc.html

- U.S. Chamber of Commerce, International Division – http://www.uschamber.com/international/default.htm

- U.S. Export Portal – http://www.export.gov

- U.S. *Export Programs Guide* – http://www.trade.gov/publications/pdfs/epg_2009.pdf

- U.S. Foreign Trade Statistics – http://www.census.gov/foreign-trade/index.html

- U.S. National Export Initiative (NEI) Site – http://www.export.gov/nei/index.asp

- U.S. State Department – http://www.state.gov

- United Nations Conference on Trade and Development (UNCTAD) – http://www.unctad.org

- Who Owns Whom Database – https://solutions.dnb.com/wow/

- World Chambers Directory – http://chamberdirectory.worldchambers.com/

- *World Factbook* – https://www.cia.gov/library/publications/the-world-factbook/index.html

References

"'Africa's Business Starts in Gauteng' – Baloyi," *Times Live,* July 31, 2010, http://www.timeslive.co.za/sundaytimes/ article578958.ece/Africas-business-starts-in-Gauteng--- Baloyi.

African Statistical Yearbook 2010. African Development Bank, 2010. http://www.afdb.org/fileadmin/uploads/afdb/Documents/ Publications/ADB_Yearbook_2010_web.pdf.

Anderson, James E., and Eric van Wincoop. "Trade Costs," *Journal of Economic Literature* 42, no. 3, (2004): 691–751.

Brinkhoff, Thomas. "Principal Agglomerations of the World," http://www.citypopulation.de/world/Agglomerations .html.

Central Intelligence Agency. "World Factbook," https://www.cia.gov/library/publications/the-world- factbook/index.html.

Financial Times. "Lexicon," http://lexicon.ft.com/.

Gladwell, Malcolm. *The Tipping Point: How Little Things Make a Big Difference.* New York: Back Bay Books, 2002.

Hofstede, Geert. "Dimensions of National Cultures," http://www.geerthofstede.nl/culture/dimensions-of-national- cultures.aspx.

Lemak, David J., and Wiboon Arunthanes. "Global Business Strategy: A Contingency Approach," *Multinational Business Review* 5, no. 1 (1997): 26–37.

Lin, Justin Y. "A Global Economy with Multiple Growth Poles" (paper presented at Korea–World Bank High Level Conference on Post-Crisis Growth and Development, Busan, Korea, June 3–4, 2010).

Osterwalder, Alexander and Yves Pigneur. *Business Model Generation: A Handbook for Visionaries, Game Changers, and Challengers*. New York: Wiley & Sons, 2010.

Porter, Michael E. "Clusters and the New Economics of Competition," *Harvard Business Review*, November–December (1998): 77–90.

Ran, Zhang, and Li Baojie. "Vuvuzela Sounds Clarion Call for Chinese Manufacturers," *Xinhua News*, June 28, 2010. http://news.xinhuanet.com/english2010/indepth/2010-06/28/c_13373262.htm.

SIL International. "Ethnologue.com," http://www.ethnologue.com/ethno_docs/distribution.asp?by=size#2.

Spulber, D.F. *Global Competitive Strategy*. Cambridge: Cambridge University Press, 2007.

"Uganda Clusters," http://www.ugandaclusters.com.

United Nations. "United Nations Population Division," http://www.un.org/esa/population/.

Wallin, Johann. *Business Orchestration: Strategic Leadership in the Era of Digital Convergence*. New York: Wiley & Sons, 2006.

About the Author

Lauri Elliott is a strategist with over 25 years of business experience, specializing in global business, innovation, technology, and new ventures and start-ups. As a noted broadcaster, author, speaker, and consultant, she helps small and medium-sized enterprises (SMEs) and entrepreneurs bring life and profit to business ideas in tough, turbulent business environments around the globe, with a particular focus on emerging markets, including Africa.

As the Director of Afribiz™ Media, Lauri has developed a solid reputation as a journalist, broadcaster, and media personality. She is the primary host of AfribizTalk™, a regular radio show about doing business and investing in Africa, and she writes frequently for publications such as *Brainstorm* magazine, an ITWeb publication, in South Africa.

In addition, Lauri is the author of *101 Leverage Points for Doing Business in Africa*, and her next books, which will be released in early 2011, are *101 Leverage Points for Doing Business in Emerging Markets* and *The Global Entrepreneur's Handbook* (http://www.globalentrepreneurhandbook.com).

To reach Lauri, visit http://www.lauri-elliott.com.